Contents

Survivors
Pitch-Black Midnight

John Goodwin

Published in association with
The Basic Skills Agency

Hodder Murray

A MEMBER OF THE HODDER HEADLINE GROUP

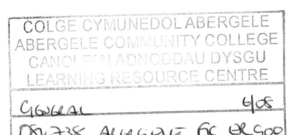
Orders: please contact Bookpoint Ltd, 130 Milton Park, Abingdon, Oxon OX14 4SB.
Telephone: (44) 01235 827720. Fax: (44) 01235 400454. Lines are open 9.00–6.00,
Monday to Saturday, with a 24-hour message answering service. Visit our website at
www.hoddereducationco.uk

© John Goodwin 2005
First published in 2005 by
Hodder Murray, a member of the Hodder Headline Group
338 Euston Road
London NW1 3BH

Impression number   10 9 8 7 6 5 4 3 2 1
Year   2010 2009 2008 2007 2006 2005

Cover photo: © Chad Ehlers/Alamy.
Illustrations by Gary Andrews.
Typeset by Transet Limited, Coventry, England.
Printed in Great Britain by Athenaeum Press Ltd, Gateshead, Tyne & Wear.

A catalogue record for this title is available from the British Library

ISBN-10: 0 340 90068 7
ISBN-13: 978 0 340 90068 0

1

Have you ever been lost in a wood?
So lost that you thought you'd never get out?
So lost that you thought you'd go mad.

Have you ever been in the pitch black?
So black that you couldn't even see
your hand in front of your face?
Not even a tiny light.
No matches or torch.

No street lights.
So black that you could hardly breathe.

I was lost in a pitch-black wood
at midnight.

It all began with a giggle.

2

Lucy giggled.
Then her giggle turned into a laugh.
A giant laugh that you could hear
ring out across the whole wood.
'Come on, Harry.
Let's crack on with the work,' she said.

I fancy Lucy something wicked.
So do all the rest of the lads.
Ben, Tariq and Jez.
She only has to wiggle her little finger.
We all come running.
We sprint and charge after her.

'Here's one,' shouted Lucy.
'It's perfect.'
'Perfect,' I repeated like a pathetic parrot.

She grabbed the long log with both hands.
Then she began to drag it across the ground.
'I'll help you,' I shouted.

Before I could move, Watson appeared.
He's our instructor.
Watson is bad news.
Big-time bad news.

'Stop there,' said Watson.
He put his foot on the log
that Lucy was moving.
'Helmets,' he said.
Lucy ignored him.
It was a bad move.
Never ignore Watson.
It doesn't pay.

Watson threw a wobbly. A mega one.
'Helmets must be worn at all times,'
he shouted.

When he'd left us, Lucy threw her helmet off.
'Load of nonsense,' she said.
Then she patted the black hat
she always wears.
It's like half a football stuffed on her head.
She never takes it off.

3

We moved the log into the space we'd cleared.
We did the same with a second log
and a third.
'It's going to be wicked,' said Lucy.
'The very best.'

We lifted two of the logs.
They leaned up against each other.
Then we lifted the third log
to balance against them.
Our shelter in the wood
was beginning to take shape.

'Now take off your T-shirt,' said Lucy.
'What for?' I asked.
'It's either that or my knickers,' said Lucy.
'And I don't fancy doing that.'

Then she began to pull at my T-shirt.
'What are you doing?' I cried.
'We need something to tie the logs together.
We haven't got any rope.
So it has to be your T-shirt.
Now get your kit off, Harry.'

My T-shirt stayed on.
So did her knickers.
We used the laces in our trainers instead.
Lucy held the top of the three logs.
I tied the laces round them tightly.
Our shelter was stronger now.

Soon it had a roof and sides.
We cut down branches from some small trees.
The leaves were our roof tiles.
Our shelter was finished.

Or so we thought.
Watson came round again.
'What's this?' he said.
He looked at the top of the logs.

'Laces from our trainers,' I said.
'Smart, isn't it?' said Lucy.

'No,' said Watson.
'It's very stupid.
I told you to use only natural things.
Stuff from the wood itself.
There isn't a trainer-lace tree
that I know of.'

Then he cut the laces with his knife
and the whole shelter collapsed.
Every single piece of it.

Lucy sent a text to Jez:

```
wot a mess
```

Jez sent a text back:

```
tuff
```

4

We tried to prop the logs up again.
But we didn't do a good job.
Watson came back.
So did the rest of the group.
'Time is up,' said Watson.

Everyone looked at our pathetic shelter.
Jez jeered and Ben laughed.
Tariq did a slow handclap.
But Watson was silent.

'We'll see Ben, Tariq and Jez's shelter now,'
said Watson.
'It's in a different clearing in the wood.'
I really didn't want to look at theirs.
But I had to.

It was huge.
They'd made a big wide doorway.
They'd built a window to look out of.
It was so tall that you could stand up in it.

'Time to test them out,' said Watson.
'The three of you get inside.'
Ben, Tariq and Jez walked into their mansion.
Watson took out a big waterpistol.

Lucy started to giggle.
He gave us two more waterpistols
from inside his rucksack.
'Wicked,' said Lucy.
She began to dance around their shelter.

Lucy fired the first squirt.
It hit Jez straight on his chin.
I landed a perfect jet of water
on the top of Ben's head.
Watson squirted all three of the lads.

After that, it was a free-for-all.
They were all soaked to the skin.

Lucy was laughing so much.
She couldn't fire straight.
But we didn't stop until all our pistols were
empty.

'What did you do that for?' said Jez.
He tipped a pool of water out of his trainer.
'It's no good if your shelter looks good
but lets the rain in,' said Watson.
'It's a waste of time.
A shelter is for survival.
Now it's the turn of you three
to test Harry and Lucy's shelter.'

Lucy dived under the branches
of our shelter.
I followed her.
Their water pistols fired
litres of water at us.
They hit the branches
and the water ran off the thick leaves
of our low shelter.

When we came out, we were perfectly dry.
No soggy clothes.
No pools of water in our trainers.

'*Now* whose shelter was the best?'
said Watson.
'It has to be Harry and Lucy's,' said Ben.
'Their shelter was waterproof.'

5

'The last part of the shelter challenge
is the hardest yet,' said Watson.
'It will be in the dark, at midnight.
You'll have to find your own way out.
Find your way back to the Centre.
You won't have any light to help you.
Leave your shelters at midnight.
You'll hear the village clock strike twelve.
Use the time now to make your plan.'

Then he left us.
Lucy and I went back to our shelter.
'It's a scary challenge,' I said.
Lucy didn't say anything.
It went very quiet.
Soon it would be dark.

'Don't you think it will be scary?' I said.
Lucy looked at me.
'You don't know what scary is,' she said.
'Don't I?' I said.
'No,' she said.
Then she reached up slowly to her hat
and pulled it off her head.
'This is scary,' she said.

On her head was a thick, long red scar.
That part of her head was completely bald.

'How did you get that?' I said.
'An accident when I was a little kid.'
'How did it happen?' I asked.
'I don't want to talk about it,' said Lucy.
'Nobody else here knows about it.
You'd better not tell them.'
'I promise I won't,' I said.

As soon as I'd said that, she kissed me.
A full, long kiss.

Then she sprang to her feet.
'Come on,' she said.
'We've got work to do.'
'What work?' I asked.
'We've got to make a plan.
We need to get out of this wood.
And we haven't got long to do it.'

Lucy sent a text to Jez:

```
wot plan u got to get out?
```

Jez sent a text back:

```
not telling u
```

6

The church clock in the far-off village
struck midnight.
'Time to move,' I said.
Lucy took hold of my hand,
and we stumbled out.
We were in the pitch-black wood.

The only sound we heard
was the crunch of small twigs under our feet.
We took one slow step at a time.
There was no moon in the sky.
Just thick blackness.
It was like we were being smothered.
We were under a dense black blanket.
Or being drowned in a black sea.

I stumbled in blind panic.

But Lucy held me steady.
'We're there,' she said.
'Reach up with your hand.'

I reached up into the empty air.
'Reach higher,' said Lucy.
I tried again.
My fingertips touched something.
I gripped it hard with both hands.
'Got it,' I said,
feeling the rough long creeper
we'd tied around the trees.
It felt like a long rope.

It was our lifeline.
By holding on to that,
we'd find our way out of the wood.

We both held on to the creeper.
We took a few steps forward.
Then a few more.
Soon we came
to Ben, Tariq and Jez's shelter.

We heard them arguing.
'This is rubbish,' shouted Tariq.
'I told you it would never work,'
screamed Jez.
'But a mobile does give you some light,'
cried Ben.
'Pathetic light,' shouted Jez.
'I can't see my hand in front of my face.'

Lucy began to giggle quietly.
I made a spooky groaning noise.
It went quiet in the lads' shelter.
'What's that?' said Jez.

We made more spooky noises.
Groans and strangled cries.
We made weird moans.

The lads cried out in panic.
Jez screamed.
Ben called out.
'Who's there?'

We didn't answer.
We left them to it.
On and on we went.
We'd tied lots of long creepers around trees.
They made one long lifeline.
Soon we'd be out of the wood.

Or so we thought.
'I can't feel the creeper any more,' I said.
'Nor can I,' said Lucy.
'It must have fallen off the tree,' I said.
'Reach down to the ground.
It must be down there,' said Lucy.

I bent down.
So did Lucy.
Lucy couldn't see me.
She fell over me.
And I fell over her.
Then she began to giggle.
It turned into a loud, long laugh.

I tried to stand up.
The bottom of my foot hit something hard.
It wasn't Lucy.
But loose gravel.

'We've hit the track,' I shouted.
'I can feel it under my foot.'
'Yeees!' said Lucy.

We walked slowly onwards.
We kept our feet on the loose gravel.

Soon there were lights showing.
The glow of the Survivors' Centre came
glittering through the dark.

Soon this survival challenge would be over.
'Were you scared in that wood?' I asked Lucy.
'No,' she said.
'I don't know what being scared is.'

We walked into the light.
What would it be like,
never to be scared again?